The Complete Guide to the Corporate Transparency Act for HOAs

By Paul K. Mengert

ISBN # 979-8-89074-740-2

Introduction

The Corporate Transparency Act (CTA) is an important piece of legislation designed to halt unlawful financial activities by enhancing the fiscal transparency of organizations and companies ... including Homeowner Associations (HOAs). This guide is intended to educate HOA, condominium, and community association leaders (these terms are used interchangeably in this article) on the evolving subject of their mandatory compliance with the CTA. The goal is to outline a) the steps to complying with the CTA, b) the impact of CTA requirements on community governance and volunteer boards, c) time frames and deadlines, d) tips and best practices, and e) future expectations.

Because the CTA is a safeguard to make sure legitimate individuals are associated with legitimate organizations, an important part of the process for HOAs is to share basic information. While the government already has this information, the CTA requires it in a certain format to link individuals with entities. Not complying with the CTA will result in costly daily financial penalties and possible prison time for willful misconduct.

The information in this paper is accurate to the best of the author's knowledge as of October, 2024, but there may be future governmental guidance, updates, or changes to the law that could impact compliance.. The best source of information on the CTA is the Financial Crimes Enforcement Network (FinCEN) website. Seek guidance from legal counsel to interpret regulations. The author cannot give legal advice; the contents of this article are strictly informational managerial guidance and not legal counsel. AI (artificial intelligence) was used to assist in research and composition in certain portions of this paper, which was then rigorously fact-checked by the author and dedicated professionals.

Table of

Contents

CHAPTER

1

The Corporate Transparency Act

An Overview

Purpose and Significance

The Corporate Transparency Act (CTA) is an important piece of crime-fighting legislation. It is designed to combat unlawful financial activities by enhancing the fiscal transparency of organizations and companies. Enacted as part of the National Defense Authorization Act for Fiscal Year 2021, the primary objective of the CTA is to prevent criminals from using anonymous shell companies for money laundering, the financing of terrorists, tax evasion, and other forms of financial crime. The CTA does this by mandating that organizations disclose Beneficial Ownership information to the Financial Crimes Enforcement Network (FinCEN). Do not be confused by the term Beneficial Owner; it will be clarified in greater detail.

The CTA is significant because it addresses a critical gap in the U.S. financial regulatory system. Prior to its enactment, the United States was limited in how it tracked the true owners of business entities, making it difficult for law enforcement and regulatory agencies to follow the money trail when investigating financial crimes. By requiring entities to report their Beneficial Owners, the CTA aims to create a robust database of basic information, increasing corporate transparency and accountability. This transparency levels the playing field for all involved parties: It helps law enforcement fight financial crime, it promotes fair business practices, and it enhances the integrity of the financial system.

Brief History and Legislative Background

The path to the enactment of the CTA was marked by extensive legislative debate and advocacy. The challenges posed by anonymous shell companies had been recognized for years. Champions for greater corporate transparency included law enforcement agencies, financial institutions, and anti-corruption organizations.

The concept of reporting Beneficial Ownership gained momentum following a number of high-profile financial scandals, such as the Panama Papers leak in 2016, which exposed the widespread use of shell companies to conceal wealth and evade taxes. These investigations underscored the urgent need for legislative action to shine a light on murky corporate ownership.

Efforts to introduce Beneficial Ownership legislation began in earnest in the early 2000s when Congress introduced several bills aimed at increasing transparency. However, these proposals faced opposition from various quarters, including business groups concerned about the regulatory burden and privacy implications.

The turning point came with the bipartisan recognition of the potential catastrophic impacts on national security. Lawmakers agreed that the lack of transparency in corporate ownership not only facilitated financial crime but also jeopardized national security by enabling terrorist financing and foreign interference in the U.S. economy.

In 2019, the Act was reintroduced in Congress with strong bipartisan support. The bill was championed by House Representatives Carolyn Maloney (D-NY) and Peter King (R-NY) and Senators Ron Wyden (D-OR) and Tom Cotton (R-AR). The proposed legislation sought to balance the need for transparency with the right to privacy, as well as the feasibility of administering the act.

The CTA was eventually incorporated into the National Defense Authorization Act (NDAA) for Fiscal Year 2021, a must-pass defense spending bill. The inclusion in the NDAA was strategic, ensuring that the CTA received the necessary legislative support for enactment. In January 2021, the NDAA, including the CTA, was passed by Congress with overwhelming bipartisan support and became law after overriding a presidential veto.

The implementation of the Corporate Transparency Act marks a milestone in the U.S.'s fight against financial crime. By mandating financial transparency through the disclosure of Beneficial Ownership information, the CTA improves the ability of law enforcement and regulatory agencies to investigate and prosecute financial crimes, and so, safeguard the integrity of the U.S. financial system and protect citizens.

CHAPTER

2

The Corporate Transparency Act and Homeowner Associations

Introduction

The Corporate Transparency Act is a pivotal piece of legislation aimed at enhancing corporate transparency and combating illicit financial activities, such as the financing of terrorism, money laundering, tax evasion, etc. Because the CTA applies to corporations, organizations, and entities, including almost all homeowner associations, it's vital that community leaders understand and comply with the Act. This chapter explores the key provisions of the CTA relevant to community associations, focusing on the definition and scope of affected organizations, as well as the reporting requirements of Beneficial Ownership.

Definition and Scope: **Organizations Covered Under the CTA**

The CTA mandates that certain entities[1,2] report their Beneficial Ownership information to the Financial Crimes Enforcement Network (FinCEN). It's important to note that the term Beneficial Owner doesn't just mean owners in the traditional sense. The CTA is designed to stop financial crimes by increasing transparency around who owns and controls companies operating within the U.S.

Community Associations and the CTA

Because HOAs are typically structured as nonprofit corporations, in most cases they are liable for the CTA's reporting requirements. The CTA covers corporations, limited liability companies (LLCs), and other similar entities that are created by filing a document with a secretary of state or a similar office under the law of a state or Indian tribe. Given that most HOAs are incorporated entities, experts believe that most are subject to the CTA.[1,2,3] However, there are exceptions.

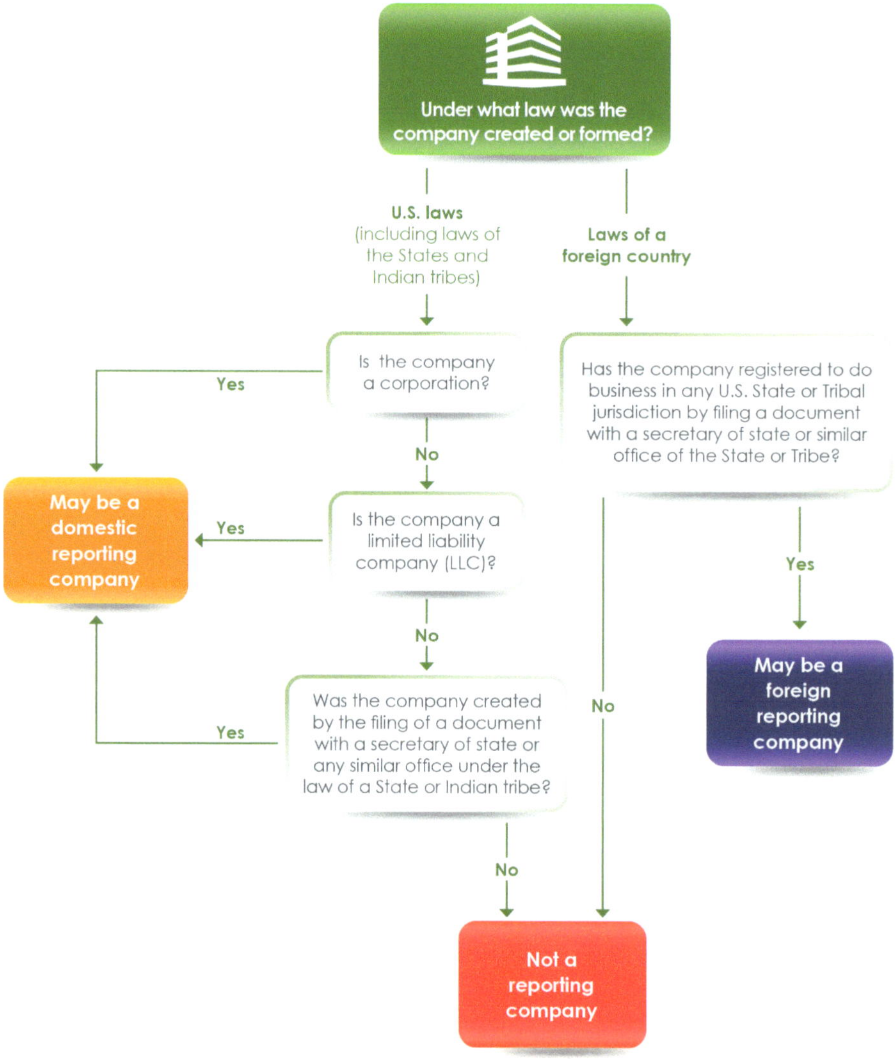

SOURCE: Beneficial Ownership Information, Frequently Asked Questions, Financial Crimes Enforcement Network, US Department of the Treasury. 2022. Updated July 24, 2024. Page 8. *https://www.fincen.gov/sites/default/files/shared/BOI-FAQs-QA-508C.pdf*

Community Associations and CTA Exceptions: **Exemptions and Exclusions**

While the CTA casts a wide net, it also provides several exemptions and exclusions to avoid heavy regulatory burdens on certain entities. Understanding these exemptions is a crucial first step for HOAs assessing their CTA compliance obligations.

Some exemptions that may apply to HOAs include:

Large Operating Companies

Entities that employ more than 20 full-time W2 employees in the U.S., conduct operations at a physical office in the U.S., and have filed a federal income tax return documenting more than $5 million in gross receipts or sales are exempt from CTA reporting. Most community associations do not meet these criteria and so do not qualify for this exemption.[4,5]

Inactive Entities

Organizations that have been in existence for over a year, have not engaged in active business, are not owned by a foreign person, and have not experienced any significant changes in ownership or assets are exempt. Some HOAs might fall under this category if they are dormant or inactive.[4,5]

Regulated Entities

Organizations already under comprehensive federal or state regulations, such as banks, insurance companies, and registered investment companies, are exempt. While community associations do not typically fall into this category, those with special regulatory oversight may want to further explore this exemption.[4,5]

501(c) Organizations

Nonprofit organizations exempt from taxation under section 501(c) of the Internal Revenue Code are not required to report Beneficial Ownership information. It is likely that some older HOAs may be exempt from the CTA requirements because they might qualify as 501(c)(4) social welfare organizations or 501(c)(3) charitable organizations. Nonprofit status can be confirmed by checking the tax return and the actual IRS 501(c) letter of acceptance. In the author's experience, few associations will meet this specific nonprofit status.[4,5]

It's important that HOAs carefully review their status to determine if they qualify for any of these exemptions. If community leaders intend not to comply because they believe the organization they represent is exempt, it is strongly recommended that they obtain guidance from their legal counsel to prevent missing important filing deadlines. Community associations that are not exempt must comply with the CTA's reporting requirements.

CTA and the Beneficial Ownership Reporting Requirement

The lynch pin of the CTA's efforts to thwart financial crimes and safeguard the public, as well as the country's financial infrastructure and national security, is the collection of information about Beneficial Owners. By law, the CTA requires organizations to report this data.

The Definition of "Beneficial Owner"

A Beneficial Owner is any individual who, directly or indirectly, through any contract, arrangement, understanding, relationship, or otherwise:

* Exercises substantial control over the entity, such as, but not limited to, a board member; or
* Owns or controls at least 25 percent of the ownership interests of the entity.[6,7]

Community Associations and Beneficial Owner Status

Because of the unique structure and governance of HOAs, defining a Beneficial Owner can be complex. Typically, community associations are governed by a board of directors elected by the member homeowners. These directors oversee the association's operations, yet they do not hold ownership interests in the traditional sense. Instead, control is exerted through their roles and responsibilities within the association.

Substantial Control

Substantial control in an HOA applies to individuals who have significant influence upon the association's decision-making and management. Individuals within a community association with substantial control may include board members or officers, such as the president, treasurer, or secretary. This includes those with authority to appoint or remove officers or a majority of the directors, important decision-makers, and any others with substantial control as defined by FinCEN.[8,9]

Ownership Interests

In most HOAs, ownership interests are distributed among the homeowners: People own a share of the association because they own property within the community. However, since no single homeowner typically owns 25 percent or more of the association, identifying Beneficial Owners based on ownership interest may not be applicable.[10,11]

SENIOR OFFICER
any individual holding the position or exercising the authority of a:
1. President
2. Chief financial officer (CFO)
3. General counsel (GC)
4. Chief executive officer (CEO)
5. Chief operating officer (COO)

or any other officer, regardless of official title, who performs a similar function as these officers

APPOINTMENT OR REMOVAL AUTHORITY
any individual with the ability to appoint or remove any **SENIOR OFFICER** or a majority of the board of directors or similar body

IMPORTANT DECISION-MAKER
any individual who directs, determines, or has substantial influence over important decisions made by the reporting company, including decisions regarding the reporting company's:

1. **Business**, such as:
   - Nature, scope, and attributes of the business
   - The selection or termination of business lines or ventures, or geographic focus
   - The entry into or termination, or the fulfillment or non-fulfillment, of significant contracts
2. **Finances**, such as:
   - Sale, lease, mortgage, or other transfer of any principal assets
   - Major expenditures or investments, issuances of any equity, incurrence of any significant debt, or approval of the operating budget
   - Compensation schemes and incentive programs for senior officers
3. **Structure**, such as:
   - Reorganization, dissolution, or merger
   - Amendments of any substantial governance documents of the reporting company, including the articles of incorporation or similar formation documents, bylaws, and significant policies or procedures

CATCH-ALL
any other form of substantial control over the reporting company. Control exercised in new and unique ways can still be substantial. For example, flexible corporate structures may have different indicators of control than the indicators included here

SOURCE: Beneficial Ownership Information, Frequently Asked Questions, Financial Crimes Enforcement Network, US Department of the Treasury. 2022. Updated July 24, 2024. Page 19. *https://www.fincen.gov/sites/default/files/shared/BOI-FAQs-QA-508C.pdf*

Information the CTA Requires Community Associations to Report

For entities covered by the CTA, the following information must be reported for each Beneficial Owner. For HOAs that are required to report under the CTA rules, Beneficial Owners are usually board members and officers who exercise substantial control over the association (or in rare cases, a homeowner who has more than a 25 percent ownership stake in the association).[6,7] The CTA requires the following information:

- Full Legal Name: The complete legal name of the Beneficial Owner.[12,13]
- Date of Birth: The individual's date of birth.[12,13]
- Residential or Business Address: The current residential or business address of the Beneficial Owner.[12,13]
- Unique Identifying Number: A unique identifying number from an acceptable document, such as a passport, driver's license, or other government-issued identification.[12,13]

CTA Compliance Process

In order to legally and accurately meet the CTA conditions, community associations must ensure they have a robust process for collecting, verifying, and reporting the required Beneficial Ownership information. This process may include:

- Establishing internal controls: Implementing procedures to identify and document individuals who meet the criteria for Beneficial Owners.
- Maintaining accurate records: Keeping detailed and up-to-date records of Beneficial Ownership information.
- Making periodic updates: Ensuring that any changes in Beneficial Ownership are reported to FinCEN promptly, as required by the CTA.[14,15]

Challenges and Considerations

It may be challenging for community associations to accurately identify Beneficial Owners due to the unique structure and the distributed nature of ownership among member homeowners. If community leaders are in doubt about the Beneficial Owners in their organization, they should consult with legal counsel and, at a minimum, create documentation of how they have established compliance. It is wise to do this for three reasons. First, an attorney can provide guidance on the interpretation of the regulations and share their experience about how other associations are complying. Second, this will lead to year-over-year consistency. Third, it could aid in a defense if the association is challenged on the accuracy of its listed Beneficial Owners. Additionally, compliance with CTA reporting requirements is non-negotiable, which means it is vital that HOAs have a clear understanding of the Act, as well as the ability to implement appropriate processes and controls to fulfill their obligations under the law.

Conclusion:
The CTA and Community Associations

Legislators believe the CTA represents a significant step toward enhancing financial transparency and combating criminal activities. Community associations can successfully navigate the complexities of this Act by understanding the exemptions and fulfilling Beneficial Ownership reporting requirements. Equally important, HOAs will contribute to the broader goal of transparency and accountability in the corporate sector, while safeguarding their own operations and governance. Of course, this will come at a cost. To fully comply with the CTA, it will be essential for many associations to seek legal counsel or professional advice. As with many regulations, the CTA is likely to add administrative and compliance costs.

CHAPTER

3

The Corporate Transparency Act

Timing and Deadlines for Homeowner Associations

Initial Reporting Requirements for HOAs

The Corporate Transparency Act mandates that certain business entities, including Homeowner Associations, report Beneficial Ownership information to the Financial Crimes Enforcement Network (FinCEN). To ensure compliance, HOAs must understand the specific timing and deadlines associated with these reporting requirements.

Effective Date and Initial Reporting for HOAs

Organizations established before January 1, 2024, including HOAs, have until December 31, 2024, to gather and submit the required Beneficial Ownership information.[16,17]

New entities created after January 1, 2024, are required to report Beneficial Ownership information upon formation or registration. This initial report must be submitted within a short timeframe, usually 30 days from the date of creation.[16,17]

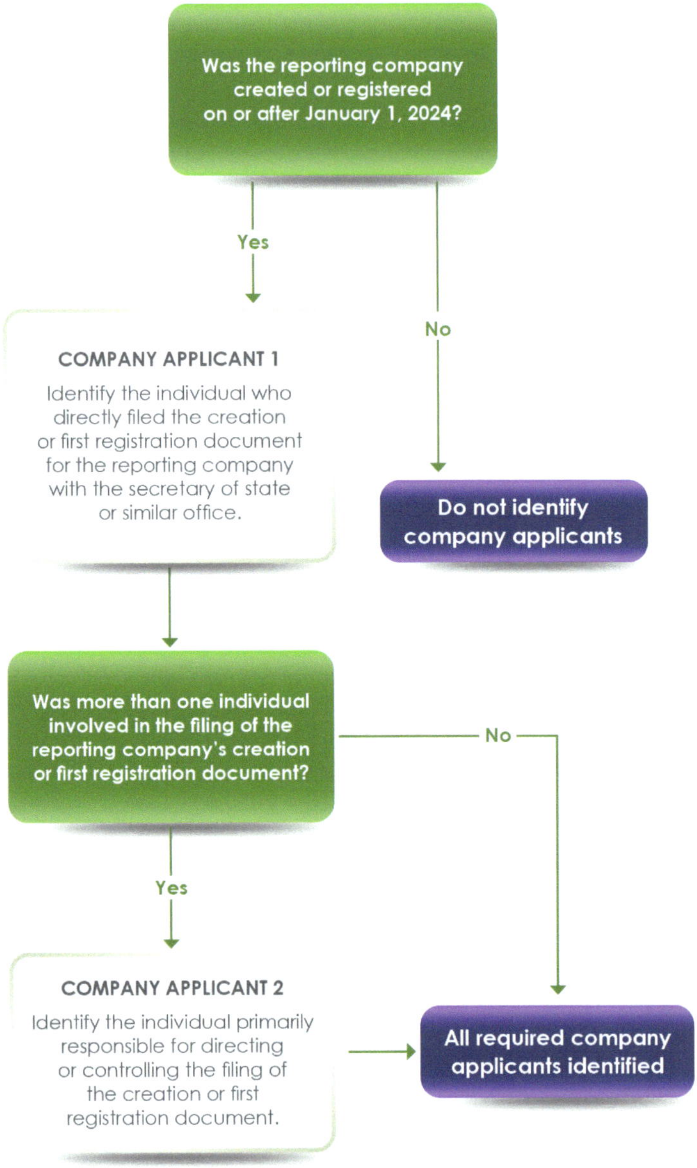

SOURCE: Beneficial Ownership Information, Frequently Asked Questions, Financial Crimes Enforcement Network, US Department of the Treasury. 2022. Updated July 24, 2024. Page 29. *https://www.fincen.gov/sites/default/files/shared/BOI-FAQs-QA-508C.pdf*

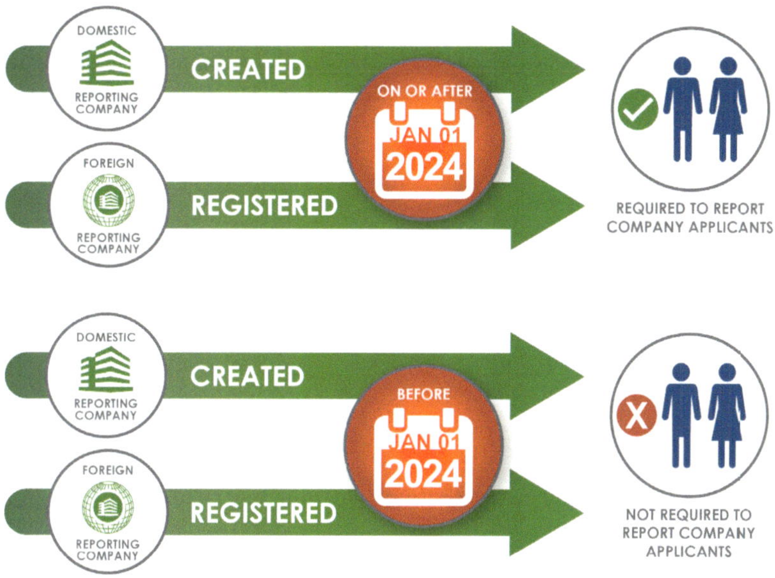

SOURCE: Beneficial Ownership Information, Frequently Asked Questions, Financial Crimes Enforcement Network, US Department of the Treasury. 2022. Updated July 24, 2024. Pages 30, 40. *https://www.fincen.gov/sites/default/files/shared/BOI-FAQs-QA-508C.pdf*

INITIAL REPORTS

Required by all companies that meet the definition of **reporting company** and are not **exempt** from that definition.

Existing reporting companies

Created or registered to do business in the United States before January 1, 2024.

Reports due by **January 1, 2025**.

New reporting companies

Created or registered to do business in the United States on or after January 1, 2024.

Reporting companies created or registered **on or after January 1, 2024** and **before January 1, 2025**, have **90 calendar days** after receiving actual or public notice that their company's creation or registration is effective to file their initial BOI reports.

Reporting companies created or registered **on or after January 1, 2025**, will have **30 calendar days** from receipt of actual or public notice that their creation or registration is effective to file their initial BOI reports.

Initial Reporting Steps for HOAs

There are three steps for reporting Beneficial Owners:

1. **Identify Beneficial Owners.**

   Community associations must identify the individuals who meet the criteria for Beneficial Ownership, focusing on those who exercise substantial control or own a significant interest in the association. These include board members, officers, people with an ownership stake of more than 25 percent, and others.[6-10]

2. **Collect Required Information.**

   Next, necessary information for each Beneficial Owner, including full legal name, date of birth, residential or business address, and unique identifying number from an acceptable identification document (driver's license, passport, etc.) must be gathered.[12,13]

3. **Submit Report to FinCEN.**

   Last, utilize the designated reporting mechanism provided by FinCEN to submit the Beneficial Ownership information within the allotted timeframe.[18,19]

Ongoing Reporting Obligations for HOAs

In addition to the initial reporting requirements, the CTA requires ongoing reports to ensure that Beneficial Ownership information remains accurate and up-to-date. It is critical that HOAs submit updates within 30 days of any changes in Beneficial Owners in order to maintain compliance and avoid inadvertently breaking the law.[14,15]

HOA Reporting of Updates and Changes

Any changes in Beneficial Ownership information must be reported to FinCEN promptly. This includes changes such as:

- Changes in Control: Changes in the individuals exercising substantial control over the HOA, such as new board members or officers, must be reported.[14,15]
- Changes in Ownership Interests: While HOAs typically have distributed ownership interests among homeowners, any significant changes that affect previously submitted information on Beneficial Ownership must be updated.[14,15]
- Changes in Identifying Information: HOAs must report any changes in the identifying information of Beneficial Owners, such as a new legal name, address, or identification documents.[14,15]

The CTA states that all changes must be reported within a specified period, usually 30 days from the date of the change.[14,15] This ensures that FinCEN's database remains current and at peak performance in its purpose of enhancing transparency and combating illegal activities.

UPDATED REPORTS

Required when there is a change to previously reported information about the reporting company itself or its beneficial owners.

Updated reports due within **30 calendar days** after a change occurs.

SOURCE: Beneficial Ownership Information, Frequently Asked Questions, Financial Crimes Enforcement Network, US Department of the Treasury. 2022. Updated July 24, 2024. Page 43. *https://www.fincen.gov/sites/default/files/shared/BOI-FAQs-QA-508C.pdf*

Annual Confirmations

While the CTA primarily focuses on initial and updated reporting, organizations may decide to confirm the accuracy of their Beneficial Ownership information annually—or more often. Confirming the data regularly ensures that entities consistently review and validate their records, promoting ongoing compliance and accountability.

Compliance Best Practices for HOAs

To effectively manage ongoing obligations for CTA reporting, HOAs should:

Implement Internal Controls

Establish robust internal procedures to monitor and track changes in Beneficial Ownership and relevant identifying information.

Maintain Accurate Records

Keep comprehensive and up-to-date records of all Beneficial Owners and any changes that occur.

Regularly Review Compliance

Periodically review compliance status and ensure that all reporting obligations are met within the required timeframes.

Conclusion: **HOAs and the CTA - Timing and Deadlines**

It is important that HOAs understand and adhere to the timing and deadlines mandated by the CTA. Legal counsel or professional advice can be invaluable in ensuring HOAs are in full compliance and avoid potential penalties. By complying with the initial reporting requirements and managing ongoing updates effectively, HOAs can contribute to the broader goal of corporate transparency and financial integrity.

CHAPTER

4

The Corporate Transparency Act

Reporting Mechanisms for Homeowner Associations

The Corporate Transparency Act requires covered entities, including Homeowner Associations, to report Beneficial Ownership information to the Financial Crimes Enforcement Network (FinCEN). This chapter explores how HOAs file reports, the timeline for reporting, confirmation and record-keeping, and the role of FinCEN.

How HOAs Can File Reports

Understanding the reporting mechanisms is crucial for HOAs to ensure compliance with the CTA. The steps to filing Beneficial Ownership information are:

Use the Electronic Filing System

FinCEN developed a secure electronic filing system for submitting Beneficial Ownership information. This system is the primary method for entities to file their reports, including HOAs. The electronic system aims to streamline the reporting process, ensuring that organizations can easily and accurately submit the required information. Third-party interfaces claiming to be more user-friendly also may be used to streamline reporting.[18,19]

Gather the Information Required

When filing reports, Beneficial Owners must provide specific information, including:

- Full legal name[12,13]
- Date of birth[12,13]
- Residential or business address[12,13]
- Unique identifying number from an acceptable identification document (passport, driver's license, or other government-issued ID)[12,13]

Follow the Step-by-Step Process

1. Access the System: HOAs will need to access FinCEN's designated online portal or a third-party interface to file the report.[18,19]
2. Enter Entity Information: Provide basic information about the HOA, including its legal name, address, and formation details.[12,13]
3. Identify Beneficial Owners: List all individuals who meet the criteria for Beneficial Ownership. Typically, this will include board members or officers who exercise substantial control, and those who own more than 25 percent of the homes, if any.[6,7]
4. Attach Documentation: Attach copies of the identification documents for each Beneficial Owner. This step assures the accuracy and legitimacy of the information provided.[12,13]
5. Review and Submit: Carefully review all entered information for correctness. Once confirmed, submit the report through the electronic filing system.[18,19]

Timeline for HOAs to Submit Reports

Initial Reporting

For existing HOAs, initial reports must be filed by December 31, 2024. New HOAs must file their reports within 30 days of formation.[16,17]

Updates

Any changes in Beneficial Ownership information must be reported within 30 days of the change.[14,15]

CORRECTED REPORTS

Required when previously reported information was inaccurate when filed and remains inaccurate.

Corrected reports due within **30 calendar days** after the reporting company becomes aware or has reason to know of an inaccuracy.

SOURCE: Beneficial Ownership Information, Frequently Asked Questions, Financial Crimes Enforcement Network, US Department of the Treasury. 2022. Updated July 24, 2024. Page 45. *https://www.fincen.gov/sites/default/files/shared/BOI-FAQs-QA-508C.pdf*

Confirmation and Recordkeeping

After submitting the report, HOAs will receive confirmation from FinCEN. It is important to keep a copy of this confirmation and maintain precise records of all submitted information for future reference and compliance audits.

FinCEN and HOAs

FinCEN plays a pivotal role in the implementation and enforcement of the CTA. As the designated agency responsible for collecting and safeguarding Beneficial Ownership information, FinCEN ensures that the collected data is properly and proficiently used to combat criminal financial activities.[20]

Key Responsibilities of FinCEN

Development of Reporting Systems

FinCEN was tasked with developing and maintaining the electronic filing system that organizations use to submit Beneficial Ownership information, including HOAs. Designed to be secure, efficient, and accessible, this system enables entities to comply with the CTA with minimal burden.[20,21]

Data Security and Confidentiality

One of FinCEN's primary responsibilities is to protect the confidentiality and security of the reported Beneficial Ownership information. The agency is required to implement stringent measures to safeguard the data against unauthorized access and misuse. This includes encryption, secure storage, and controlled access protocols to allow only authorized personnel to access the information.[20,21]

Information Verification and Analysis

FinCEN will verify the completeness and accuracy of all submitted reports. This process may involve cross-referencing the information HOAs provide with other databases and records to confirm its legitimacy. Additionally, FinCEN will analyze the data to identify patterns and trends that could indicate potential financial crimes.[20,21]

Collaboration with Law Enforcement

In an effort to uphold the nation's financial integrity and transparency, FinCEN works with various law enforcement agencies and regulatory bodies to share Beneficial Ownership information, as needed. This collaboration is essential for investigating and prosecuting cases of money laundering, terrorist financing, and other financial crimes.[20,21]

Guidance and Outreach

FinCEN is responsible for providing guidance and support to entities, including HOAs, to help them understand and comply with the CTA. FinCEN facilitates accurate and complete reporting by issuing detailed instructions, conducting training sessions, and offering technical assistance to organizations.[21]

Conclusion: **HOAs and Reporting Mechanisms**

The reporting mechanisms under the CTA are designed to ensure that Beneficial Ownership information is accurately and securely collected, stored, and used. For HOAs, understanding how to file reports and the role FinCEN plays in the successful completion of the filing process is essential for compliance. By utilizing FinCEN's secure electronic filing system and adhering to the reporting timelines, community associations can fulfill their obligations under the CTA and help improve financial transparency and fight illegal activities.

CHAPTER

5

The Corporate Transparency Act

Compliance and Enforcement for Homeowner Associations

The Corporate Transparency Act requires certain entities, including most Homeowner Associations, to report Beneficial Ownership information to the Financial Crimes Enforcement Network (FinCEN). HOA compliance with the CTA is critical to avoid significant penalties and to assist in assuring the nation's financial transparency and integrity. This chapter examines the compliance obligations of HOAs, the penalties for noncompliance, and best practices for implementing effective compliance programs.

Four Steps Existing HOAs Need to Take to Comply with the CTA

Step 1.

Identify Beneficial Owners

First, HOAs must identify individuals who meet the criteria for Beneficial Ownership, focusing on those who exercise substantial control or have significant ownership interests. Typically, this includes board members and others who meet the criteria.[6,7]

Step 2.

Collect Required Information

HOAs must see to it that each Beneficial Owner registers and submits specific information, including their full legal name, date of birth, residential or business address, and a unique identifying number from an acceptable identification document (passport, driver's license, government ID, etc.).[12,13]

Step 3.

Submit Initial Reports

After the information on all the Beneficial Owners is filed, the HOA will submit an initial report to FinCEN through the designated electronic filing system. Existing HOAs have until December 31, 2024, to comply. New HOAs must submit their reports within 30 days of formation.[16,17]

Step 4.
Report All Changes

Any changes to Beneficial Ownership information must be reported within 30 days. This includes changes in control, ownership interests, or identifying information.[14,15]

The Role of HOA Governance in Ensuring CTA Compliance

Board of Directors

The board of directors plays an important part in ensuring compliance with the CTA. They must oversee the identification and reporting processes, ensuring that accurate and complete information is submitted.

Compliance Officer

Appointing a compliance officer can help the HOA streamline the CTA compliance process. This individual would be responsible for monitoring compliance activities, maintaining records, and ensuring timely submission of reports.

Training and Awareness

Regular training sessions on the CTA's requirements for HOA board members and officers can help ensure everyone is aware of their responsibilities. This includes understanding what constitutes Beneficial Ownership and the importance of accurate reporting.

Internal Policies

Developing internal policies and procedures that outline the steps for identifying and reporting Beneficial Ownership information can help HOAs maintain compliance. These policies should include guidelines for record-keeping, verifying information, and reporting timelines.

Civil and Criminal Penalties Applicable to HOAs

HOAs that do not comply with CTA requirements can face severe penalties, both civil and criminal. Understanding the penalties for not adhering to this important law is essential for HOAs.

Civil Penalties

- Failure to file accurate and timely reports can result in civil penalties of up to $500 per day for each day the violation continues.[22,23]
- Civil penalties can accumulate quickly for noncompliant HOAs, leading to substantial financial burdens.

Criminal Penalties

- Willful failure to file reports or the submission of false or fraudulent information can result in criminal penalties, including fines of up to $10,000 and imprisonment for up to two years.[22,23]
- Individuals responsible for submitting false information may face personal liability and criminal charges.[22,23]

Due Diligence and Best Practices: Implementing an Effective HOA Compliance Program

Proper preparation prevents poor performance—*and* penalties. Due diligence in regards to the CTA begins with an effective HOA compliance program.

Develop a Compliance Framework

Establish a comprehensive compliance framework that includes policies, procedures, and internal controls to ensure HOA adherence to the requirements of the CTA. This framework should outline the responsibilities of board members and the compliance officer.

Conduct Regular Training and Education

Maintain a culture of compliance by conducting regular training sessions for HOA board members and officers to keep them informed about their compliance obligations and any updates to the CTA.

Monitor and Review

Regularly review HOA compliance activities and procedures to make sure they are productive. Conduct periodic audits to help identify gaps or areas for improvement in the compliance program.

Internal Controls and Recordkeeping Tailored for HOAs

It is said, the devil is in the details. So is heaven. Run a tight compliance ship with fine-tuned internal controls and assiduous recordkeeping.

Accurate Recordkeeping

Maintain detailed and accurate records of all HOA Beneficial Ownership information. This includes documentation of the identification process, submitted reports, and any updates. Proper recordkeeping is fundamental in demonstrating compliance in case of an audit or investigation.

Regular Updates

Establish a system for regularly updating HOA Beneficial Ownership information. This includes setting reminders for periodic reviews and reporting any changes within the required timeframe.[14,15]

Risk Management

Assess the risks associated with HOA noncompliance with the CTA and develop strategies to mitigate these risks. This may include conducting risk assessments and implementing additional controls to address identified vulnerabilities.

Conclusion: HOAs and CTA Compliance and Enforcement

Compliance with the CTA is essential for HOAs to avoid significant penalties and to be a part of the nation's effort to promote financial transparency and integrity. By understanding their compliance obligations and implementing internal best practices, due diligence, and a culture of accountability and continuous improvement, HOAs can successfully comply with the CTA.

CHAPTER

6

The Corporate Transparency Act

Implications and Impact on Homeowner Associations

The Corporate Transparency Act has broad implications for Homeowner Associations, affecting their operations, legal status, and financial services, as well as their role in the global context of property management. This chapter explores these impacts in detail, focusing on the effects of the CTA on HOAs and the international context.

Impacts: Changes to HOA Operations and Practices

The CTA will require HOAs to adopt new operational practices in order to comply with the reporting requirements of Beneficial Ownership. Compliance is likely to be extensive and expensive, but will vary depending on the size and structure of the HOA.

Administrative Burden

HOAs must allocate resources to identify Beneficial Owners,[6,7] collect required information,[12,13] and submit reports to FinCEN.[18,19] This administrative burden can be significant, especially for small HOAs with limited staff and resources. Larger HOAs may need to establish a dedicated compliance officer or hire additional staff to manage the increased workload.

Policy Development

HOAs will need to develop and implement new policies and procedures for identifying and reporting Beneficial Ownership information. These policies should include clear guidelines for collecting, verifying, and updating information. Regular training and education for board members and officers will be necessary, so that everyone understands their responsibilities under the CTA.

Recordkeeping and Reporting

Accurate recordkeeping is foundational to compliance. HOAs must maintain detailed records of Beneficial Ownership information, as well as any changes to that information. This includes documentation of the identification process and submitted reports. HOAs should establish systems for regular updates and periodic reviews to ensure ongoing compliance with the CTA.

Challenges and Considerations for Small vs. Large HOAs

CTA requirements for reporting Beneficial Ownership are a vital tool in safeguarding U.S. financial systems and citizens against crime. While HOAs are an important part of this mission, they must be prepared for the impact of this law on the allocation of association resources.

Small HOAs

Small HOAs often operate with limited budgets and staff, making compliance with the CTA particularly challenging. The administrative burden of identifying Beneficial Owners and submitting reports may strain resources. These HOAs may need to seek support from legal counsel or compliance consultants to meet their obligations.

Large HOAs

Larger HOAs may have more resources but they also may face greater complexity in compliance. They must manage a larger number of Beneficial Owners and may have more intricate governance structures. These HOAs are likely to establish dedicated compliance teams and implement sophisticated recordkeeping and reporting systems to manage their obligations effectively.

Compliance Costs

Compliance with the CTA may increase operational costs for HOAs. These costs include administrative expenses, legal fees, and potential payments associated with hiring compliance officers or consultants. Financial advisors can help HOAs budget for these additional expenses and identify possible funding sources to cover compliance costs.

Risk Management

Financial advisors are good partners in helping HOAs manage the risks associated with noncompliance. Tactics for minimizing risk include developing risk management strategies and implementing internal controls to ensure ongoing compliance with the CTA. Advisors must stay informed about changes in regulations and provide timely updates to HOAs to mitigate potential compliance risks.

Conclusion: CTA Implications and Impacts for HOAs

While HOAs are an important cog in the wheel of the fight against financial crime, it's equally important for them to meet the CTA requirements with a good plan and able partners. Planning and partnership can help HOAs assess the impact of compliance, manage the risk of noncompliance, and wisely allocate the resources needed to obey the law.

CHAPTER

7

The Future of the Corporate Transparency Act and Homeowner Associations

The Corporate Transparency Act represents a significant step toward increasing transparency in business ownership. However, as with any major legislation, future developments and potential amendments are likely. This chapter explores possible legislative changes and the implications for Homeowner Associations.

Potential Amendments, Updates, and Changes

As the CTA is implemented and its impacts are assessed, various stakeholders, including lawmakers, regulatory bodies, and industry groups, may propose amendments to address emerging issues and enhance the Act's effectiveness. Potential areas for legislative changes include:

Clarification of Beneficial Ownership Definitions

As HOAs and other entities work to comply with the CTA, ambiguities in and confusion over the definition of Beneficial Ownership may arise.[6,7] Future legislative updates might seek to clarify these definitions to promote consistent and accurate reporting. Specific amendments could be introduced to provide more detailed criteria for what constitutes "substantial control"[8,9] and "ownership interests"[10,11] in the context of different types of entities, including HOAs.

Adjustment of Reporting Thresholds

Lawmakers may consider adjusting the thresholds for reporting Beneficial Ownership information. For example, they may revise the current 25 percent ownership[10,11] threshold based on feedback from enforcement agencies and compliance experts. While lowering the threshold could enhance transparency by increasing the number of individuals required to report, it might also increase the compliance burden for HOAs and other entities.

Expansion of Exemptions

The CTA includes several exemptions for certain types of entities.[4,5] Future amendments might expand these exemptions to include additional categories of organizations that demonstrate a low risk of being used for illicit activities. For HOAs, this could mean the introduction of specific exemptions or streamlined reporting requirements for small or low-risk associations.

Enhanced Privacy Protections

Because Beneficial Ownership information is sensitive, there may be calls for stronger privacy protections to prevent misuse or unauthorized access. Legislative updates could introduce more robust data security measures and access controls. These enhancements would help address concerns about the confidentiality and safety of the reported information, particularly for individuals in high-profile or vulnerable positions.

Integration with Other Regulatory Frameworks

The CTA could be integrated more closely with other regulatory frameworks, both domestically and internationally. This integration might involve coordinating reporting requirements with existing Anti-Money Laundering (AML) and Counter-Terrorism Financing (CTF) regulations. This could simplify compliance for HOAs by aligning CTA requirements with other reporting obligations associations might already be subject to, reducing duplication of effort.

Implications of Future Change for HOAs

It is said, the only thing certain is change. It can also be said that the only thing certain *about* change is that it can cause more work and requires more planning and preparation. HOAs need to be prepared for the impacts of future legislative and other changes to the CTA.

Increased Compliance Burden

Amendments that lower reporting thresholds or expand the scope of the CTA could increase the compliance burden for HOAs. These changes would require HOAs to identify and report additional Beneficial Owners, necessitating more resources and effort. In particular, smaller HOAs might need to invest in compliance tools or seek outside partners, such as legal counsel or compliance experts, to effectively manage these increased responsibilities.

Enhanced Transparency and Accountability

Legislative updates aimed at clarifying definitions and expanding exemptions[4,5] could enhance the transparency and accountability of HOAs. Clearer guidelines would help HOAs understand their obligations and ensure accurate reporting. Increased transparency can also strengthen the governance of HOAs, building trust among members and stakeholders.

Privacy and Data Security Concerns

Stronger privacy protections would address concerns about the safety of Beneficial Ownership information. HOAs must stay informed about new data security requirements and update their compliance measures accordingly.

Adaptation to Global Standards

Amendments that align the CTA with international standards could affect HOAs managing cross-border properties. Some HOAs may need to adapt their compliance programs to meet both domestic and international requirements. Staying informed about global regulatory developments will be crucial for these HOAs to maintain compliance and avoid potential legal and financial repercussions.

Ongoing Education and Training

As legislation changes, continuing education and training for HOA board members and officers will be essential. Keeping up with evolving requirements ensures that HOAs remain compliant and can proficiently manage their reporting obligations. Providing regular updates and training sessions can help HOAs handle changes and maintain robust compliance programs.

Conclusion: **The Future of the CTA and HOAs**

In the future, the Corporate Transparency Act will likely see several amendments and updates aimed at refining its provisions and improving its effectiveness. Homeowner Associations must stay informed about these potential changes and actively adapt their strategies to maintain compliance with the law.

CHAPTER

8

Technological Advances in Homeowner Association Compliance and Corporate Transparency

As Homeowner Associations navigate the complexities of the Corporate Transparency Act, many find that leveraging technology can play a crucial role in improving compliance and corporate transparency. This chapter explores how technology can facilitate HOA compliance and examines future trends in corporate transparency for property management.

Ways Technology Can Improve HOA Compliance

Streamlines Date Collection and Reporting

Technology solutions can significantly streamline the process of collecting and reporting Beneficial Ownership information.[12,13] Advanced software platforms designed for compliance can automate data collection, verification, and reporting, reducing the administrative burden on HOAs. A big benefit of platforms is that they may be integrated with existing HOA management systems, allowing seamless data transfer and minimizing the risk of errors. Plus, automated reminders and alerts ensure that deadlines for initial and ongoing reporting are met. While these solutions may help HOAs stay compliant with the CTA, they also will introduce new costs.

Enhances Recordkeeping and Documentation

Digital recordkeeping systems provide a secure and organized way to store Beneficial Ownership information. These systems encrypt sensitive data to protect confidentiality and prevent unauthorized access. Implementing a centralized digital repository allows HOAs to easily access and update records for compliance audits and reviews. These systems also facilitate version control, ensuring that the most current information is always available.

Manages Compliance

Comprehensive compliance management software can help HOAs track their CTA reporting obligations, as well as other regulatory requirements. These solutions offer dashboards and reporting tools that provide real-time insights into compliance status. These tools enable HOAs to identify and address potential compliance gaps, reducing the risk of noncompliance and associated penalties.

Supports Training and Education

E-learning platforms and webinars can provide user-friendly, up-to-date training for HOA board members and officers. These resources cover the latest regulatory changes, best practices for compliance, and practical tips for managing reporting requirements. Interactive training modules and quizzes can help reinforce learning, so that all stakeholders understand their responsibilities under the CTA.

For more information, check out the podcast on the CTA:
https://www.hoacommunityleaders.com/corporate-transparency-act

and other resources at
www.amgworld.com/CTA.

Conclusion: Technology - The CTA and HOAs

Technology can be a powerful tool to improve HOA compliance with the Corporate Transparency Act. Adopting advanced compliance management solutions, improving data security, and leveraging emerging technologies can streamline compliance processes and foster transparency. As future trends in corporate transparency continue to evolve, HOAs must stay informed and adapt to new technological advancements to maintain regulatory compliance and contribute to the fiscal integrity of the property management sector.

The Corporate Transparency Act has generated significant discussion within the property management industry, particularly among Homeowner Associations. While the CTA aims to enhance financial transparency and prevent criminal activities, it can be problematic from the perspective of industry stakeholders. This chapter explores common criticisms and challenges HOAs face in complying with the CTA and concludes with an industry perspective.

Common Criticisms and Challenges Faced by HOAs

Administrative Burden

One of the most frequently cited criticisms of the CTA is the increased administrative burden that it imposes on HOAs. The tasks of identifying Beneficial Owners,[6,7] collecting necessary information,[12,13] and submitting reports[14-17] require significant time and resources. Smaller HOAs may struggle to allocate sufficient resources to meet these demands.

Cost of Compliance

Compliance with the CTA can be expensive, especially for HOAs with limited budgets. Costs related to hiring compliance officers, retaining legal counsel, and implementing compliance management systems can add up. These expenses can be heavy for small and mid-sized HOAs that operate on tight budgets.

Complexity of Reporting Requirements

The reporting requirements are challenging. Determining who qualifies as a Beneficial Owner in the context of an HOA can be difficult due to the unique governance structures of associations. HOAs must carefully work through the intricate definitions and complicated criteria of the CTA to ensure accurate reporting.

Privacy Concerns

Many HOAs and their members are concerned about the privacy implications of the CTA. Reporting Beneficial Ownership information involves sharing sensitive personal data, which raises red flags about data security and potential misuse. Protecting confidentiality and preventing exposure of this data is a major challenge.

Uncertainty and Ambiguity

Despite the CTA's clear objectives, there are areas of ambiguity and uncertainty in its implementation. HOAs often find themselves trying to clarify specific aspects of the law, such as more details about the criteria for Beneficial Ownership and possible expansion of the scope of exemptions. This lack of clarity can lead to compliance delays and increased legal costs.

Impact on Volunteer Boards

Many HOAs are managed by volunteer boards that may lack the expertise and experience needed to complete complex regulatory requirements. The CTA adds another layer of responsibility for these volunteers, who must now ensure that their association complies with federal regulations.

Industry Response: The CTA and HOAs

While everyone agrees that the goal of the CTA is a noble one, not everyone agrees with the reach and scope of the legislation. HOA stakeholders have a different vision for how the CTA should apply to associations.

Calls for Exemptions

Industry stakeholders, including HOA advocacy groups, have called for exemptions or streamlined reporting requirements for HOAs. They argue that the risk of illicit financial activities within HOAs is relatively low compared to other types of entities. Plus, the regulatory burden may be disproportionate.

Request for Clarifications

There is a strong demand for clearer guidance and detailed instructions from regulatory authorities. HOAs are governed by volunteers from all walks of life—they are not legislative professionals or legal scholars. HOAs seek more precise definitions and criteria so volunteers fully understand their obligations under the CTA. Industry groups have requested that FinCEN provide additional resources and support to assist HOAs in compliance.

Support for Compliance Assistance

In response to the challenges faced by HOAs, some industry groups are advocating for the development of compliance assistance programs. These programs would offer training, resources, and technical support to help HOAs meet their reporting obligations effectively and efficiently.

Emphasis on Data Security

The industry has highlighted the need for robust data security measures to protect the sensitive information HOAs will collect under the CTA. Stakeholders urge regulatory authorities to prioritize data protection and implement stringent safeguards to prevent unauthorized access and breaches.

Conclusion: **Industry Feedback and Criticisms**

While all agree with the intent of the CTA, the implementation of the Act presents several challenges for HOAs, ranging from increased administrative burdens and costs of compliance to concerns over privacy and data security. Industry stakeholders have responded by advocating for exemptions, clearer guidance, compliance assistance programs, and stronger data security measures. These responses are designed to help HOAs meet their obligations under the CTA, while minimizing the impact on their operations and resources. As the CTA evolves, ongoing dialogue between regulatory authorities and industry stakeholders will be crucial in addressing these concerns and refining the regulatory framework.

CHAPTER

10

The Corporate Transparency Act and Homeowner Associations: Conclusion

The Corporate Transparency Act represents a significant regulatory shift aimed at improving financial transparency and fighting illegal activities. While its objectives are clear, the CTA poses several challenges for Homeowner Associations, including increased administrative burden, heavy costs of compliance, complexity of reporting, privacy concerns, and uncertainties surrounding requirements.

Future Changes and Immediate Compliance

As the CTA continues to be implemented, future amendments and updates are likely to address some of these challenges. Potential legislative changes may include clarifications of Beneficial Ownership, clearer definitions, adjustments to reporting thresholds, and better privacy protections. These changes will strive to balance the need for transparency with the practical realities faced by HOAs.

However, despite the possibility of future changes, HOAs must comply with the CTA's current requirements to avoid hefty fines and possible criminal charges. Noncompliance can result in significant financial penalties and adverse legal consequences for both the association and its board members.[22,23]

Industry Initiatives

The property management industry is actively working to support HOAs in traversing the complexities of the CTA. Advocacy groups are pushing for exemptions and streamlined reporting requirements for low-risk entities, such as HOAs. Additionally, there are calls for more comprehensive compliance assistance programs to provide HOAs with the resources and support needed to fulfill their obligations.

Immediate Steps for HOAs

Step 1.
Develop Compliance Programs

HOAs should establish strong compliance programs that include detailed policies and procedures for identifying and reporting Beneficial Ownership information.[6,7,12,13]

Step 2.
Leverage Technology

Utilizing advanced compliance management solutions can help HOAs streamline data collection, improve reporting, and enhance record-keeping processes.

Step 3.
Seek Professional Guidance

Legal counsel and compliance experts can deliver valuable assistance to HOAs navigating the CTA's requirements, with the end goal of ensuring accurate reporting.

Step 4.
Stay Informed

HOAs must stay updated on regulatory developments and potential legislative changes that may affect their compliance obligations. By taking these steps, HOAs can assure compliance with the CTA, mitigate risks, and contribute to the broader goals of financial transparency and integrity. It is hoped that industry collaboration and ongoing advocacy will result in future regulatory adjustments that will better accommodate the unique characteristics of and challenges faced by Homeowner Associations. The commitment to immediate compliance to current regulations, despite the anticipation of future changes, underscores the importance of maintaining the credibility and legal standing of HOAs.

References

1. Small Entity Compliance Guide, Beneficial Ownership Information Reporting Requirements. Financial Crimes Enforcement Network, US Department of the Treasury. Version 1.1. December, 2023. Pages 2-3. *https://www.fincen.gov/sites/default/files/shared/BOI_Small_Compliance_Guide.v1.1-FINAL.pdf*

2. Beneficial Ownership Information, Frequently Asked Questions, Financial Crimes Enforcement Network, US Department of the Treasury. 2022. Updated July 24, 2024. Pages 4-5. *https://www.fincen.gov/sites/default/files/shared/BOI-FAQs-QA-508C.pdf*

3. Beneficial Ownership Information, Frequently Asked Questions, Financial Crimes Enforcement Network, US Department of the Treasury. 2022. Updated July 24, 2024. Page 9. *https://www.fincen.gov/sites/default/files/shared/BOI-FAQs-QA-508C.pdf*

4. Small Entity Compliance Guide, Beneficial Ownership Information Reporting Requirements. Financial Crimes Enforcement Network, US Department of the Treasury. Version 1.1. December, 2023. Pages 4-14. *https://www.fincen.gov/sites/default/files/shared/BOI_Small_Compliance_Guide.v1.1-FINAL.pdf*

5. Beneficial Ownership Information, Frequently Asked Questions, Financial Crimes Enforcement Network, US Department of the Treasury. 2022. Updated July 24, 2024. Page 6. *https://www.fincen.gov/sites/default/files/shared/BOI-FAQs-QA-508C.pdf*

6. Small Entity Compliance Guide, Beneficial Ownership Information Reporting Requirements. Financial Crimes Enforcement Network, US Department of the Treasury. Version 1.1. December, 2023. Page 16. *https://www.fincen.gov/sites/default/files/shared/BOI_Small_Compliance_Guide.v1.1-FINAL.pdf*

7. Beneficial Ownership Information, Frequently Asked Questions, Financial Crimes Enforcement Network, US Department of the Treasury. 2022. Updated July 24, 2024. Pages 12, 19. *https://www.fincen.gov/sites/default/files/shared/BOI-FAQs-QA-508C.pdf*

8. Small Entity Compliance Guide, Beneficial Ownership Information Reporting Requirements. Financial Crimes Enforcement Network, US Department of the Treasury. Version 1.1. December, 2023. Pages 17, 20. *https://www.fincen.gov/sites/default/files/shared/BOI_Small_Compliance_Guide.v1.1-FINAL.pdf*

9. Beneficial Ownership Information, Frequently Asked Questions, Financial Crimes Enforcement Network, US Department of the Treasury. 2022. Updated July 24, 2024. Pages 12-14. *https://www.fincen.gov/sites/default/files/shared/BOI-FAQs-QA-508C.pdf*

10. Small Entity Compliance Guide, Beneficial Ownership Information Reporting Requirements. Financial Crimes Enforcement Network, US Department of the Treasury. Version 1.1. December, 2023. Pages 18, 21, 22. *https://www.fincen.gov/sites/default/files/shared/BOI_Small_Compliance_Guide.v1.1-FINAL.pdf*

11. Beneficial Ownership Information, Frequently Asked Questions, Financial Crimes Enforcement Network, US Department of the Treasury. 2022. Updated July 24, 2024. Page 15. *https://www.fincen.gov/sites/default/files/shared/BOI-FAQs-QA-508C.pdf*

12. Small Entity Compliance Guide, Beneficial Ownership Information Reporting Requirements. Financial Crimes Enforcement Network, US Department of the Treasury. Version 1.1. December, 2023. Page 38. *https://www.fincen.gov/sites/default/files/shared/BOI_Small_Compliance_Guide.v1.1-FINAL.pdf*

13. Beneficial Ownership Information, Frequently Asked Questions, Financial Crimes Enforcement Network, US Department of the Treasury. 2022. Updated July 24, 2024. Pages 28-29. *https://www.fincen.gov/sites/default/files/shared/BOI-FAQs-QA-508C.pdf*

14. Small Entity Compliance Guide, Beneficial Ownership Information Reporting Requirements. Financial Crimes Enforcement Network, US Department of the Treasury. Version 1.1. December, 2023. Pages 45-47. *https://www.fincen.gov/sites/default/files/shared/BOI_Small_Compliance_Guide.v1.1-FINAL.pdf*

15. Beneficial Ownership Information, Frequently Asked Questions, Financial Crimes Enforcement Network, US Department of the Treasury. 2022. Updated July 24, 2024. Pages 29, 35-38. *https://www.fincen.gov/sites/default/files/shared/BOI-FAQs-QA-508C.pdf*

16. Small Entity Compliance Guide, Beneficial Ownership Information Reporting Requirements. Financial Crimes Enforcement Network, US Department of the Treasury. Version 1.1. December, 2023. Pages 33, 35, 42. *https://www.fincen.gov/sites/default/files/shared/BOI_Small_Compliance_Guide.v1.1-FINAL.pdf*

17. Beneficial Ownership Information, Frequently Asked Questions, Financial Crimes Enforcement Network, US Department of the Treasury. 2022. Updated July 24, 2024. Page 3. *https://www.fincen.gov/sites/default/files/shared/BOI-FAQs-QA-508C.pdf*

18. Small Entity Compliance Guide, Beneficial Ownership Information Reporting Requirements. Financial Crimes Enforcement Network, US Department of the Treasury. Version 1.1. December, 2023. Page 43. *https://www.fincen.gov/sites/default/files/shared/BOI_Small_Compliance_Guide.v1.1-FINAL.pdf*

19. Beneficial Ownership Information, Frequently Asked Questions, Financial Crimes Enforcement Network, US Department of the Treasury. 2022. Updated July 24, 2024. Pages 3-4. *https://www.fincen.gov/sites/default/files/shared/BOI-FAQs-QA-508C.pdf*

20. Small Entity Compliance Guide, Beneficial Ownership Information Reporting Requirements. Financial Crimes Enforcement Network, US Department of the Treasury. Version 1.1. December, 2023. Page xi. *https://www.fincen.gov/sites/default/files/shared/BOI_Small_Compliance_Guide.v1.1-FINAL.pdf*

21. Beneficial Ownership Information, Frequently Asked Questions, Financial Crimes Enforcement Network, US Department of the Treasury. 2022. Updated July 24, 2024. Pages 1-2, 48-49. *https://www.fincen.gov/sites/default/files/shared/BOI-FAQs-QA-508C.pdf*

22. Small Entity Compliance Guide, Beneficial Ownership Information Reporting Requirements. Financial Crimes Enforcement Network, US Department of the Treasury. Version 1.1. December, 2023. Page 15. *https://www.fincen.gov/sites/default/files/shared/BOI_Small_Compliance_Guide.v1.1-FINAL.pdf*

23. Beneficial Ownership Information, Frequently Asked Questions, Financial Crimes Enforcement Network, US Department of the Treasury. 2022. Updated July 24, 2024. Page 39. *https://www.fincen.gov/sites/default/files/shared/BOI-FAQs-QA-508C.pdf*

Acknowledgments

I wish to express my deepest gratitude to Dacy Cavicchia, Adriana Moreno, Joselin Paz, Melanie Raskin, and AI for their (and its!) meticulous and insightful contributions to this guide. Their collective expertise and attention to detail in research, composition, and editing have been invaluable throughout this process. Each of these contributions was instrumental in shaping and refining the content of this work.

About the Author

Entrepreneur, speaker, and author, Paul K. Mengert, is the founder and CEO of Association Management Group. With decades of experience in the community management arena, he earned both the Certified Manager of Community Associations and Professional Community Association Manager designations. A natural teacher, both as an industry leader and volunteer, Paul shares his wealth of knowledge about business and community management as a Community Associations Institute National Faculty Member lecturer at Wake Forest Law School, a teacher for the Harvard Business School Alumni of Charlotte program at Queens University, and a frequent speaker at conferences, such as CAI's National Conference and Law Seminar. Active in his community and dedicated to sustainable community growth and health, he is the Chairman of the Piedmont Triad International Airport Board and former Chair of the North Carolina Legislative Action Committee Board.